DATE DUE

22404

PRIMARY SOURCES OF EVERYDAY LIFE IN COLONIAL AMERICA™

Home Life in Colonial America

Charlie Samuel

The Rosen Publishing Group's
PowerKids Press™
New York

Published in 2003 by The Rosen Publishing Group, Inc.
29 East 21st Street, New York, NY 10010

First Edition

Photo Credits: Key: t: top, b: below, c: center, l: left, r: right
p.4cl Corbis/Bettmann; p.4b Mary Evans Picture Library; p.4tl Peter Newark's American Plctures; p.7 Angelo Hornak; p.8cr American Museum, Bath; p.8tl Christie's Images; p.8b Angelo Hornak; p.11 Corbis/Philadelphia Museum; p.11b Peter Newark's American Pictures; p.12tl Christie's Images; p.12 bl Mary Evans Picture Library; p.12cr Angelo Hornak; p.15 Peter Newark's American Pictures ; p.16tr Corbis/Historical Picture Archive; p.16cr Bridgeman Art Library/American Museum, Bath; p.19tl American Museum, Bath; p.19tr Ecoscene; p.19bl Mary Evans Picture Library; p.20tl Angelo Hornak; p.20b Art Archive/New York Public Library.

Library of Congress Cataloging-in-Publication Data

Samuel, Charlie.
   Home life in colonial America / Charlie Samuel.
      v. cm. – (Primary sources of everyday life in colonial America)
Includes bibliographical references and index.
Contents: A new country – Colonial housing: From shelters to homes – Furniture in colonial homes – Colonial families – Children in the colonies – Working around the house – Spinning, weaving, and sewing – Colonial food and drink – Colonial cooking – Changing lifestyles.
   ISBN 0-8239-6599-6 (library binding)
   1. United States–Social life and customs–To 1775–Juvenile literature. 2. Home–United States–History–Juvenile literature. [1. United States–Social life and customs–To 1775.]
I. Title. II. Series.

E188 .S19 2003
306'.0973–dc21

                                    2002004484

Contents

▶ John Smith, a leading colonist, drew this map of New England in 1616. It shows English settlements along the coast.

▼ English colonists in America included Puritans and other religious groups who were banned in England.

▼ The Pilgrims give thanks after landing in America in 1620. The sea journey from Europe took up to four months. Some people died on the way.

A New Country

After 1492, when Europeans heard about America, they began to set up communities there called **colonies**. The Spanish set up colonies in Mexico and the Southwest. French colonies began in what is now Canada and in Louisiana, a territory that lay west of the Mississippi River. From 1607 on, the English, Swedish, and Dutch settled on the east coast of North America. By 1669, the English claimed 13 colonies that stretched along the coast from New Hampshire, in the north, to Georgia, in the south.

Life was hard for the colonists. America was not like Europe. The northern colonies were very cold in the winter. The southern colonies were too hot in the summer. There were different plants and different animals. At first the settlers struggled to survive, but slowly they began to live more like they had in Europe. Some colonists got help from Native Americans. Other Native Americans thought the Europeans were stealing their land, and attacked them.

Colonial Housing: From Shelters to Homes

The first settlers needed shelter. Some copied the homes of Native Americans. They made a cage of thin branches covered with thatch or tree bark. Others dug holes in banks where they made a house from upright logs. They put mud between the logs to keep out the wind. There was no glass, so windows were small. After 1638, Scandinavian settlers in Delaware began to build cabins from logs laid on top of one another with a roof of **thatch**. The log cabin became the most common home for European settlers when they first moved into a new region.

Within a century, colonial houses were more like homes in Europe. Most were made of wood and had only one floor and two or three rooms. Richer settlers built large homes using brick. In New England, homes were often made of clapboard, or overlapping planks. In the South, wealthy homes had verandas so that people could sit outside.

▼ This is a modern copy of the first kind of log homes built by the colonists. Huts were often dug into a bank of earth to make them more sturdy.

▼ By the eighteenth century, rich colonists built themselves large, comfortable homes. This house was built on the James River in Virginia between 1723 and 1770.

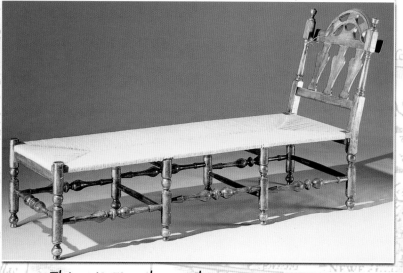

◄ This is a daybed from the eighteenth century. People could sit or lie on it. It was made in Philadelphia, but the style was English.

► This picture shows three colonial beds, an adult's bed, a small bed that fits underneath it, and a baby's crib.

▼ This room shows how furniture looked in the 1600s. There is a high chair for a baby (left) and a simple table.

Furniture in Colonial Homes

It was difficult for the first settlers to bring furniture from England. Instead they cut down trees and used the wood to make chairs and tables. The woodworkers were not very skilled. They made simple chests for storing belongings, and benches and stools on which to sit. People slept on settles, which were wooden couches that folded out to make beds.

As the colonies grew, American craftsmen became more skilled. They copied European styles, but their work remained simple. Some wealthy Americans still preferred to buy their furniture from Europe rather than from America. They thought it was made better. People also believed that the furniture from Europe was more tasteful than the pieces made in America.

It was only in the eighteenth century that skilled American **cabinetmakers** began to create a style of their own, instead of copying designs from Europe. Carpenters began making items such as cupboards, writing desks, and chests of drawers.

Colonial Families

Most colonists had families. Only about three settlers in one hundred did not get married. Families were an important source of support. They shared jobs in the house and on the land. They provided company for one another. They looked after each other when they were sick.

Some early colonists, such as the Puritans of New England, brought their whole families to America. South of Chesapeake Bay, however, most settlers were young men. There were not many women for them to marry. Families there only became common in the eighteenth century.

Fathers were the heads of colonial families. Wives and children had to obey the man of the house. Many colonists died young, so men and women whose partners died often married for a second or third time.

Family life for colonial slaves was difficult. Their real families were split up if they were bought and sold. Some slaves formed communities that acted like families, caring for one another.

▶ *This portrait shows a Dutch family in the early seventeenth century. Families were often very strict. Fathers kept order, and parents dressed their children like small adults.*

▼ *This Puritan family is listening to a reading from the Bible. Worshiping together was important for colonists who belonged to religious groups.*

◄ This picture shows a young American boy in the eighteenth century. Babies wore long gowns, but boys and girls dressed like adults. They often wore clothes that had been passed down by their older brothers and sisters.

► This nursery was created late in the eighteenth century in Massachusetts. By then children were allowed more time to play with toys such as rocking horses, dolls, and tea sets.

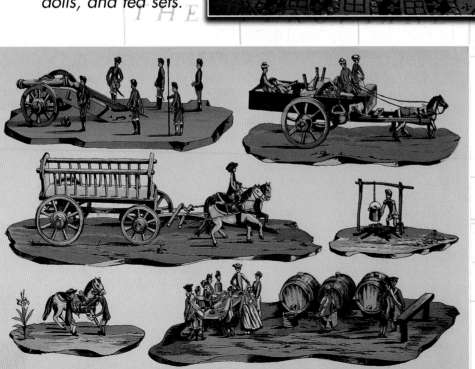

◄ There were very few toys in the early colonies. Most toys were brought to America from Europe. These drawings show toy soldiers and other figures that came from France.

Children in the Colonies

Colonists had large families. Many children died from diseases such as smallpox, so people had more children than they do today. Many settlers thought that children had to be treated strictly to make them good citizens. Parents beat children who misbehaved. People expected children to act, and even to dress, as little adults.

Most young children studied at home with their parents. After the first teacher arrived in America in 1635, some older children went to school. All children did chores in the house. When they were 9 or 10, boys left home to learn a trade as an **apprentice**. Sometimes they learned how to shoot so that they could join the **militia**. Girls became maids or cooks. Work did not leave much time for playing. Children did, however, play games such as hopscotch and leapfrog.

From around 1750, parents began to treat their children more as parents do today. They spent more time playing with, and caring for, their children, instead of being so strict.

Working Around the House

Most colonial families had very busy lives. There was lots of work to do. Men and women had different jobs. Men often worked at trades, such as carpentry, hunting, or farming, to get food for their families. Women looked after the house. They cooked meals and made clothes. They kept everything clean, and washed and ironed clothes. They also cared for the family garden and made medicines from herbs and other plants. Children helped their fathers and mothers with jobs.

Rich colonists had slaves or **indentured servants** to help them in the house and on the land. More than one half of all colonists came to America as indentured servants. They worked hard in their homes and on the land. Most servants were men from ages 15 to 25. In return for the cost of the trip to America, servants agreed to work for a master for a period of time, usually between four and seven years. At the end of that time, they were free to leave.

▶ Women did all the domestic chores, such as laundry and cooking, as well as looking after the young children. Men did not do housework. They worked on the land or had a trade.

▼ This idealistic painting of a frontier home does not show what life was really like. Women and children often had to work hard. Food was not always as plentiful as the hunters' heavy load suggests.

◄ *This woman is using a spinning wheel (left) to twist wool fibers into yarn. She then loops the yarn onto a large turning frame (right).*

► *Women stitched patterns onto pieces of cloth called samplers. This sampler was made in New Hampshire.*

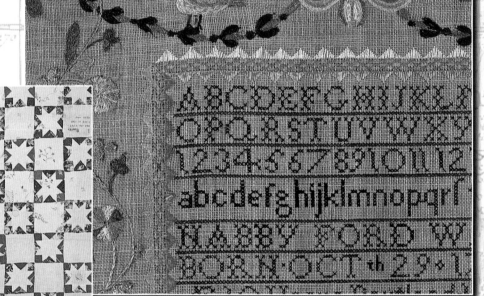

◄ *To make quilts, women sewed two layers of cloth together with a thick padding between them. The padding made quilts very warm for bedding.*

Spinning, Weaving, and Sewing

Making cloth was important work. Colonists needed cloth to make clothes, blankets, and rugs. Most people used a simple, rough cloth called homespun. In 1634, a Massachusetts law stopped colonists from using expensive **textiles** like lace or silk. Colonial officials thought that expensive cloth was a sign that a person was proud or wasteful.

The colonists grew flax to make linen. They raised sheep to get wool. They used animal skins to make clothes out of fur and leather.

Originally, men made most of the cloth. However, women soon learned the skill of weaving. Eventually women made nearly all of the cloth. They spun fibers of flax or sheep's wool to make long threads of yarn. Then they wove the yarn into pieces of cloth to sew together. Cloth was valuable for trading with other colonists. Families could exchange pieces of cloth for other goods or for food.

Colonial Food and Drink

When Europeans first arrived in America they found many plants and animals that they did not know. They had never seen corn, for example, or squash, or a turkey. Some friendly Native Americans showed the settlers how to plant and grow corn. Corn grew better in the colonies than did many European crops, and it became the colonists' most important food. People later took corn and squash to Europe to grow them there.

Wealthy colonists ate the same kinds of food wealthy people ate in Europe. In addition to their regular meals, they could enjoy treats such as butter, muffins, and jam. Ordinary settlers were not so lucky. Their main meal, at midday, consisted of a stew of meat and vegetables or, if they lived by the coast, seafood and vegetables.

At home colonists drank fruit juice or milk. Tea was also a popular drink. Men usually drank beer and hard cider in taverns. The colonists tried to make wine from grapes. It was not very good wine, but grape juice became popular.

▲ This ring-shaped bottle was made from decorated pottery. It held a drink called switchel. Switchel was made from sugar, ginger, molasses, vinegar, and water.

▲ Pumpkins and other types of squash did not grow in Europe. Colonists in America learned from Native Americans that squash were good to eat, and also learned the best ways to cook them.

◄ These wealthy eighteenth-century Americans are drinking tea. Tea was a very popular drink in England at the time, and colonists brought the habit to America.

◀ This is the kitchen of a large house in Virginia in the early 1700s. In wealthy homes, the slaves or servants did the cooking and other chores.

▼ These Native Americans are cooking fish and meat, including lizards, on a barbecue. Colonists learned a lot about food from Native Americans.

Colonial Cooking

Women and their children did the cooking in colonial homes. Most colonists did not have many pots and pans in which to cook different meals. Iron pots were expensive to buy. Many meals were "one-pot" meals, meaning that all the ingredients were cooked together in a stew in a single pot. The stews were often cooked in a brick oven. Some colonists learned how to dig a hole in the ground and light a fire in it from the Native Americans. They put a lid on their stewpot and put it in the pit. The heat from the fire slowly cooked the food.

Cooks did not have many different **ingredients**. Most **recipes** used standard ingredients, such as beans, pork, and corn. Meals often tasted the same each day. Colonists learned from Native Americans what spices made food taste better. Colonists began to use mace, cinnamon, cloves, and ginger. In the Spanish colonies in the South and Southwest, hot red chili or cayenne pepper were popular spices.

Changing Lifestyles

The colonies became independent from British rule when they won the **American Revolution**, which was fought between 1775 and 1783. By that time, colonists had learned the best ways to farm in America. Even poor colonists had more to eat than poor people in Europe. Better food helped to make the colonists more healthy. In 1775 Americans were on average 1 or 2 inches (2.5–5 cm) taller than were Europeans.

More Americans lived in large towns than ever before. In 1775, for example, 30,000 people lived in Philadelphia. Town life was different from the lives of earlier colonists. People lived close to their neighbors in brick row houses. They had more people to **socialize** with rather than just their families. There were more jobs in towns. There were more stores, which sold all kinds of goods. During the American Revolution, people were proud to buy American goods from stores. Colonists wanted to show that they were ready to break away from their European roots.

Glossary

American Revolution (reh-vuh-LOO-shuh) The war that American colonists fought from 1775 to 1783 to win independence from England.

apprentice (uh-PREN-tis) An inexperienced person learning a skill or trade.

cabinetmakers (KAB-nit MAY-kurs) Skilled workmen who make wooden furniture.

colonies (KAH-luh-neez) New places where people move, but are still ruled by the old country's leaders.

indentured servants (in-DEN-churd SUR-vintz) People who work for another person or other people for a fixed amount of time for payment of travel or living costs.

ingredients (in-GREE-dee-untz) The different foods a cook uses to make a dish.

militia (muh-LIH-shuh) A group of people who are trained and ready to fight in an emergency.

recipes (REH-sih-peez) Instructions for how to cook various dishes.

socialize (SOH-shul-eyz) To seek out the company of others.

textiles (TEKS-tylz) Cloths made by knitting or weaving yarn or thread into a fabric.

thatch (THACH) A material made from straw or grass used to make roofs.

Index

Primary Sources

Page 4 (top right). Map of New England, drawn by John Smith in 1614. **Page 7 (bottom).** Shirley Plantation House stands on the James River in Virginia. **Page 8 (top).** William and Mary style daybed made in Philadelphia in the eighteenth century. **Page 8 (center).** Colonial bedroom, reconstruction at the American Museum, Bath, United Kingdom. **Page 8 (bottom).** Seventeeth-century colonial "keeping" room reconstructed at the American Museum, Bath, United Kingdom. **Page 11 (top).** *Portrait of Anthony Reyniers and his Family*, painted in 1631 by Cornelis de Vos. The painting is now in the Philadelphia Museum of Art. **Page 11 (bottom).** Family Bible reading, engraving made by E. A. Abber in September 1883. **Page 12 (top).** Portrait of young boy, 18th century, no details. **Page 12 (center).** Nursery room of a Massachusetts house, late eighteenth century. **Page 16 (top).** Woman Skeining Wool, watercolor painting. **Page 16 (bottom right).** This sampler with birds and flowers was embroidered in New Hampshire in the eighteenth century. **Page 16 (bottom left).** This quilt was made in America during the colonial period. **Page 19 (top left).** Pottery switchel bottle from colonial America. **Page 20 (top).** Restored eighteenth-century kitchen at Shirley Plantation, James River, Virginia.

Web Sites

Due to the changing nature of Internet links, PowerKids Press has developed an online list of Web sites related to the subject of this book. This site is updated regularly. Please use this link to access the list: www.powerkidslinks.com/pselca/hlca.